SEP   2011

Slavery in America

JEAN F. BLASHFIELD

Children's Press®
An Imprint of Scholastic Inc.
New York Toronto London Auckland Sydney
Mexico City New Delhi Hong Kong
Danbury, Connecticut

Content Consultant
James Marten, PhD
Professor and Chair, History Department
Marquette University
Milwaukee, Wisconsin

Library of Congress Cataloging-in-Publication Data

Blashfield, Jean F.
  Slavery in America/Jean F. Blashfield.
     p. cm. — (A true book)
  Includes bibliographical references and index.
  ISBN-13: 978-0-531-26311-2 (lib. bdg.)   ISBN-13: 978-0-531-26624-3 (pbk.)
  ISBN-10: 0-531-26311-8 (lib. bdg.)   ISBN-10: 0-531-26624-9 (pbk.)
  1. Slaves—United States—History—Juvenile literature. 2. Slavery—United States—History—
Juvenile literature. 3. Slave Trade—United States—History—Juvenile literature. 4. Plantation
life—United States—History—Juvenile literature. 5. United States—History—Civil War, 1861–
1865—African Americans—Juvenile literature. I. Title.
  E441.B64 2011
  306.3'620973—dc22   2011010399

All rights reserved. Published in 2012 by Children's Press, an imprint of Scholastic Inc.
Printed in China 62
SCHOLASTIC, CHILDREN'S PRESS, A TRUE BOOK, and associated logos are trademarks and/or
registered trademarks of Scholastic Inc.
1 2 3 4 5 6 7 8 9 10 R 21 20 19 18 17 16 15 14 13 12

Find the Truth!

Everything you are about to read is true *except* for one of the sentences on this page.

Which one is **TRUE**?

T or F The first African slaves in the Americas lived in Virginia.

T or F Civil War battles took place in almost every part of the country.

Find the answers in this book.

Contents

THE **BIG** TRUTH!

Newly arrived slaves

4

Slaves on a cotton plantation

NARRATIVE
OF THE
LIFE
OF
FREDERICK DOUGLASS,
AN
AMERICAN SLAVE.

WRITTEN BY HIMSELF.

BOSTON:
PUBLISHED AT THE ANTI-SLAVERY OFFICE,
No. 25 CORNHILL.
1846.

Frederick Douglass changed his name
from Frederick Augustus Washington
Bailey after escaping slavery.

The first enslaved Africans in Virginia arrive at Jamestown on a Dutch ship.

6

CHAPTER 1

Slavery in the Colonies

Slavery has existed in some form throughout all of history. Roman, Greek, and African cultures had slavery in ancient times. In the Americas, Spanish explorers took enslaved Africans to Central America and the Caribbean as early as 1501. Less than 100 years later, the Spanish took slaves to Florida. The first Africans in the colonies were also slaves. In 1619, a Dutch ship arrived at Jamestown carrying 20 Africans. The captain traded them for food.

Enslaved Africans were brought into early Jamestown to work on tobacco farms.

In the North

Europeans flocked to claim land in the northern section of North America. To encourage settlement, England offered additional land to any Englishman who imported a worker into an English colony. Yet few people were willing to come over simply to work someone else's land. To acquire workers, many colonists brought in slaves and **indentured** servants. Indentured servants agreed to work for four to seven years in exchange for transportation to America.

Dutch colonists attend New Amsterdam's first slave market in 1655.

8

New York's first slave market was opened at Wall Street in 1711.

The Dutch at New Amsterdam, today's New York, began to bring in slaves in 1626. Over the years, New Amsterdam became a market for slaves. Ships brought Africans there. They were then sold and sent to other colonies. Most northern colonial households that owned slaves usually had at least two. They did the housework and helped in small businesses. These first slaves were probably freed after a few years. Gradually, northerners began to see less need for slaves.

Native Americans as Slaves

Before Europeans arrived, Native American groups kept war captives from other native groups as slaves. Usually, they either traded slaves to other groups or took them into their own societies. They sometimes sold their slaves to white settlers. But it was easy for a Native American slave to escape captivity and not be recognized as a runaway. As African slaves became more available in the colonies in the 1700s, the trade of Native American slaves ended.

Colonists transport a captured Native American to a slave ship.

The Colonial South

In the South, slaves were vital to the economy. They worked on **plantations**, large farms that produced a single crop, such as tobacco, rice, sugar, or cotton. Buying and maintaining slaves required a minimal amount of money. Slaves became the cheapest and most efficient form of labor. As a result, many plantation owners became very wealthy. Enslavement usually lasted a person's entire life. Even children born to slaves were enslaved.

George Washington owned 316 slaves at the time of his death.

CHAPTER 2

The Slave Trade

The international slave trade started in Africa, where members of one people would attack another and turn their captives into slaves. The Portuguese found that many Africans would sell their slaves to white people. They set up trading posts along the west coast of Africa. Soon the British, Dutch, and French also began to take part in the slave trade.

An estimated 13 percent of slaves died while sailing the Middle Passage.

The Triangle Trade

The international slave route formed a triangle across the Atlantic Ocean. Europeans shipped manufactured items to Africa, where the goods were traded for slaves. Slaves were shipped to the English, Spanish, and Portuguese colonies in the Americas, where they grew sugar, tobacco, and other crops. Those crops were shipped to Europe. The middle part of the triangle, through which slaves crossed the Atlantic, was called the Middle Passage.

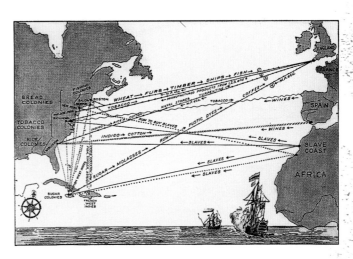

This map shows routes taken by ships along the triangle of trade in the 17th century.

Slavers tried to fit as many humans into a ship as possible. The slaves were kept chained in place. Many died during the journey, which could last two or three months. Disease spread easily through the crowded ship and often killed captives. Others died while fighting against their captors on the ship.

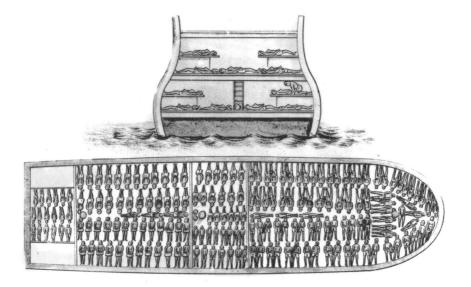

This drawing shows how captives were organized on slave ships to make room for as many people as possible.

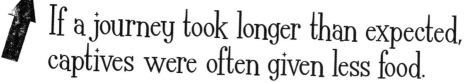
If a journey took longer than expected, captives were often given less food.

These traders, however, knew that they would make more money if their human cargo arrived in good condition. When captives died, it meant the traders lost some income. Therefore, captives who were kept below decks were occasionally taken on deck to exercise. Slavers also gave their captives food and water twice a day.

Outlawing the Importation of Slaves

When the U.S. Constitution was written in 1787, it stated that the government could not ban the importation of slaves for 20 years. In 1807, the United States and Great Britain outlawed the slave trade completely. By that time, at least 12 million Africans had been taken from Africa to the Western Hemisphere. It is estimated that more than 50,000 ship crossings were made.

As many as 12 million Africans were brought to the Americas and enslaved.

Slavers advertised ahead of time, letting people know they would be arriving with a cargo of new slaves for sale.

This group of slaves stands in front of buildings on a Beaufort, South Carolina plantation in 1862.

Even after slaves were no longer being imported, the number of slaves in the United States increased. This happened because an enslaved woman's children were also considered slaves.

CHAPTER 3

The Lives of Slaves

Some owners had one slave, who worked in both the house and vegetable garden. Others owned 100 or more slaves to do the work on a big plantation.

Owners usually did not spend much money on food, clothes, and housing for their slaves. Slaves worked long days. They were generally given enough to eat, but the food lacked the vitamins and minerals needed to stay healthy. Their houses, or quarters, were simple and crowded.

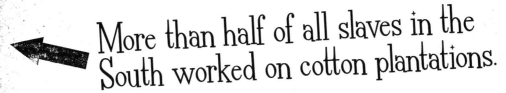

More than half of all slaves in the South worked on cotton plantations.

Rice planters paid more for slaves who came from rice-growing countries or regions.

An overseer watches as slaves work on a North Carolina rice plantation.

How Were Slaves Treated?

Slaves usually had to work from sunrise to sunset. They worked even longer during harvest time. Slaves might work in the fields or in the owner's home. In the fields, they were ordered and supervised by a field boss or an **overseer**. In the house, the owner's wife ordered the tasks. All states had Slave Codes, which outlined the limited rights of slaves. These codes usually gave owners absolute control over their human property.

Slaves could be whipped or placed in stocks. Stocks were devices that held a person's hands, head, or feet, keeping the person in a very uncomfortable position. Slaves could also be branded, or marked, with a hot iron. Sometimes owners were taken to court for mistreating their slaves, but they were rarely found guilty. Many slaves felt that the only positive future was escape or death.

Stocks have been used as a form of punishment around the world for centuries.

A woman and her children, chained together, are sold to a new owner.

Selling Humans

A misbehaving slave might be sold, as if he were any other piece of property. Frequently, a slave family was broken apart. A woman and her children might be sold and separated from the father. A father or sibling might be sold. As children grew up, they might be sold more than once. Slaves were also sometimes given away as gifts. Separated families often never found each other again.

Slaves were at times auctioned off. Prospective buyers could inspect them, looking for health or strength, depending on the kind of work the slaves would be doing. Slaves were then sold to the person willing to pay the most.

As the soil in states such as Virginia, Kentucky, and North Carolina wore out, slaves there were sold elsewhere. Many were sold to landowners to work the fields in Mississippi and Texas.

A good field-worker could cost $1,500 at auction in 1850, or around $42,500 today.

The Children

It took many slaves to work the plantations. Slave owners expected the women to have several children. The owners needed the children to replace older slaves who became sick or died. A woman working as a slave in the fields continued to work even while she was pregnant. After she gave birth, she had to carry the baby on her back into the fields.

Children began working in the field at an early age.

A slave assisted George Washington during Washington's early days as a surveyor.

At about age five, children began working. By the time they were 12, they did the same work as adults. Some younger slaves in the house were allowed to learn to read with the white children they cared for. Slaves who were considered intelligent by their owners were sometimes taught to be carpenters, surveyors, or accountants. These slaves might even earn small amounts of money.

The Underground Railroad

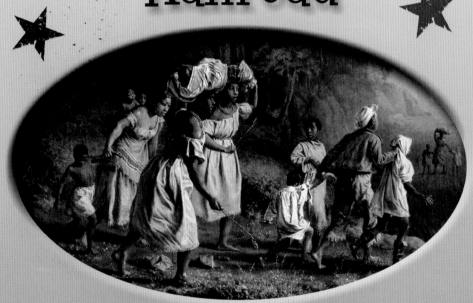

The Underground Railroad was a system of routes used by slaves running away from the South. It began to develop in the early 19th century. The system was most active from 1850 to 1860, leading up to the Civil War.

A series of U.S. laws required people to return **fugitive**, or runaway, slaves to their owners. As a result, fugitives had to go all the way to Canada to reach safety. The journey could take many months. They traveled by night and often had to hide in basements and tunnels during the day.

Harriet Tubman, a fugitive slave from Maryland, returned to the South many times to help others escape. Her efforts to help fugitives reach freedom earned her the nickname Moses.

Some people hid fugitive slaves in their houses. These houses often had hidden spaces under the floor or behind cabinets and shelves where fugitives could hide.

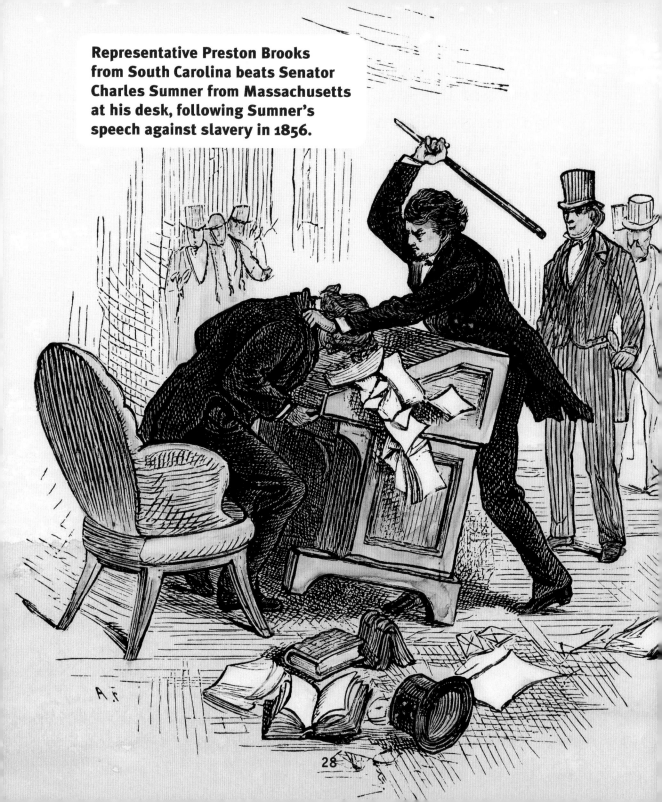

Representative Preston Brooks from South Carolina beats Senator Charles Sumner from Massachusetts at his desk, following Sumner's speech against slavery in 1856.

CHAPTER 4

The Beginning of the End

Many people wanted to **abolish**, or do away with, slavery. In 1777, Vermont outlawed slavery in its new constitution. One by one, other northern states began to follow Vermont's example.

But slavery had become too important to the economy of the South for owners to free their slaves. Additionally, southern states held a lot of power in the U.S. Congress. The South would not easily be forced to follow the North's **emancipation** of slaves.

Southerners in Congress tried to stop Northerners from discussing antislavery ideas. 29

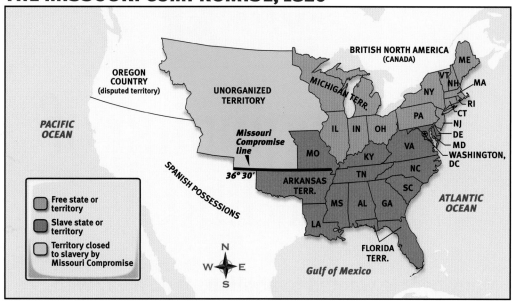

This map shows which states and territories allowed slaves and which did not. New states north of the line could not have slaves.

Division

Congress passed the Missouri **Compromise** in 1820. It allowed Maine to be admitted to the Union as a non-slave, or free, state. Missouri was admitted as a slave state. This kept an equal number of free and slave states in the Union. Yet debate continued as more territories worked to become states.

Northerners wanted a federal law to decide which future states would be free or slave. Southerners wanted each state to decide for itself.

In 1850, Congress passed the Fugitive Slave Law. It required all captured runaway slaves to be returned to their owners. Many escaped slaves told northerners how difficult their lives were in the South. Their stories were often printed in newspapers and widely read. The number of northerners who supported abolition grew. Meanwhile, the North and South were moving further apart on the issue of slavery.

NARRATIVE

OF THE

LIFE

OF

FREDERICK DOUGLASS,

AN

AMERICAN SLAVE.

WRITTEN BY HIMSELF.

BOSTON:
PUBLISHED AT THE ANTI-SLAVERY OFFICE,
No. 25 CORNHILL.
1846.

Frederick Douglass published his experiences in 1846, eight years after escaping slavery.

Crowds gather in Montgomery, Alabama, to watch Jefferson Davis being sworn in as president of the Confederate States of America.

CHAPTER 5

The Fight to End Slavery

In 1860, Abraham Lincoln was elected president. Lincoln generally opposed slavery. Southern states feared he would eventually have it abolished. Over the next few months, eleven states **seceded** from, or left, the Union. They formed the **Confederate** States of America. Northern states insisted that they had no right to separate from the United States. The two sides went to war. From 1861 to 1865, Northerners and Southerners fought each other in the American Civil War.

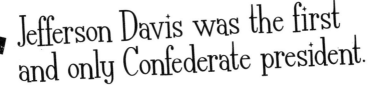

Jefferson Davis was the first and only Confederate president.

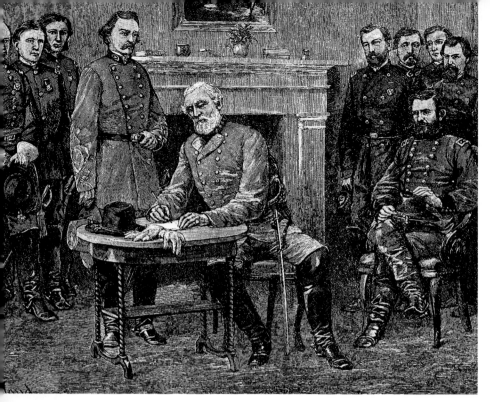

General Lee's surrender at Appomattox, Virginia, marked the beginning of the end of the Civil War.

620,000 Americans died during the Civil War.

The Battles

Southern armies won several battles early in the war. But as the war raged on, the North began winning more major battles. Fighting took place in almost every part of the country, even as far west as Arizona. On April 9, 1865, the South surrendered to Northern leaders at Appomattox, Virginia.

The Emancipation Proclamation

In 1862, President Lincoln announced a plan. All slaves in Confederate territory would be emancipated, or freed, unless states returned to the Union by January 1, 1863. No state returned, so the Emancipation Proclamation took effect. As Northern armies took control in Southern states, they freed the slaves. The former slaves were poor and had no place to go. But they were free to make their own choices.

Union soldiers lead newly freed slaves to freedom and safety in Union territory.

African Americans in the War

Some slaves fought to defend their Southern owners and their homes. Many of these slaves died.

Other slaves sought protection with Northern troops. They were called **contrabands**. They found their way to U.S. troops, knowing they would not be returned to their masters.

Timeline of Slavery in America

1619
The first slaves are brought to Jamestown.

1808
Slaves could no longer be imported into the United States.

January 1, 1863
The Emancipation Proclamation frees slaves in Confederate states.

Contrabands often wanted to join the Union army. Since 1792, however, it had been illegal for blacks to bear arms for the U.S. Army. In 1863, the law was changed. By the end of the war, about 180,000 blacks served in the army. Another 19,000 served in the navy.

1870

The 15th Amendment guarantees males the right to vote regardless of race.

1865

The 13th Amendment frees all slaves.

38

CHAPTER 6

Freedom

The newly freed slaves had to find ways to support themselves. Most had no education and could only farm. Some former slaves had help getting land or starting businesses. Many worked as paid servants for their former owners. They were often paid only with a share of the crop they planted. Others moved west. Thousands went to Kansas, the Dakotas, and Nebraska, where they could **homestead** new land.

After the war, schools were established in some places in the South to help former slaves receive an education.

A Time of Political Power

In 1870, the 15th Amendment to the U.S. Constitution guaranteed all male citizens, including African Americans, the right to vote. Not only did many African Americans vote, but some also ran for political office. After the war, several African Americans were elected to serve in Congress. The first in the U.S. Senate was Hiram R. Revels of Mississippi. Joseph Rainey of South Carolina was the first elected to the U.S. House of Representatives.

This portrait shows the first African Americans to be voted into Congress after the 15th Amendment was approved. Hiram Revels is at the left.

During Reconstruction, former slaves started a town in Virginia called Freedman's Village.

The early years after the war were called Reconstruction. The states that had seceded rebuilt their towns and businesses, and wrote new state constitutions. Each Southern state that seceded had to meet certain conditions to reenter the Union. In 1866, Tennessee was the first state to reenter. Four years later, in 1870, Texas became the last. U.S. troops left the South by 1877.

Supporters of the civil rights movement of the 1950s and 1960s used nonviolent, or peaceful, protest.

People hold signs in protest of separate white and African American schools.

A Long Struggle

After Recontruction, former Confederate states began to pass laws that limited African Americans' freedoms. Many were denied the right to vote. Schools for African Americans were separate and often not as good as local white schools. Many of these laws remained in effect until the 1960s. Although slavery has been outlawed for almost 150 years, its impact on the nation's history continues to this day. ★

True Statistics

Number of Africans brought to America: About 645,000

Colonists who made the first stand against slavery: Quakers in Pennsylvania in 1688

Number of slaves in America when it became the United States: About 700,000

Population of the new United States: 3.9 million

Number of African Americans free in 1790: 60,000

Number of slaves living in the South in 1860: More than 3.1 million

Number of slaves who escaped to Canada on the Underground Railroad: About 30,000

Number of African Americans who died fighting in the Civil War: About 38,000

Did you find the truth?

F The first African slaves in the Americas lived in Virginia.

T Civil War battles took place in almost every part of the country.

Resources

Books

Fradin, Dennis Brindell. *The Underground Railroad*. New York: Marshall Cavendish, 2012.

Grant, Reg. *Slavery: Real People and Their Stories of Enslavement*. London: Dorling Kindersley, 2009.

Haskins, James, and Kathleen Benson. *Following Freedom's Star: The Story of the Underground Railroad*. New York: Benchmark Books, 2002.

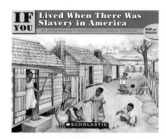

Kamma, Anne, and Pamela Johnson. *If You Lived When There Was Slavery in America*. New York: Scholastic, 2004.

Landau, Elaine. *Slave Narratives: The Journey to Freedom*. New York: Franklin Watts, 2001.

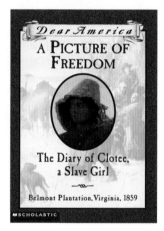

McKissack, Patricia. *A Picture of Freedom: The Diary of Clotee, a Slave Girl—Belmont Plantation, Virginia 1859*. New York: Scholastic, 2003.

Rossi, Ann. *Freedom Struggle: The Anti-Slavery Movement 1830-1865*. Washington, DC: National Geographic, 2005.

Organizations and Web Sites

Aboard the Underground Railroad
www.cr.nps.gov/nr/travel/underground/states.htm
Learn about the slave trade, the antislavery movement, the Underground Railroad, and the Civil War.

Slavery and the Making of America, a PBS series
www.pbs.org/wnet/slavery
Read about the history and geography of slavery in America, which formed the basis for the PBS television series.

Places to Visit

Charles H. Wright Museum of African American History
315 East Warren Avenue
Detroit, MI 48201
(313) 494-5800
www.chwmuseum.org
Check out the exhibits and programs that explore African American history.

National Underground Railroad Freedom Center
50 East Freedom Way
Cincinnati, OH 45202
(513) 333-7500
www.freedomcenter.org
Learn the stories about freedom's heroes, from the era of the Underground Railroad to present times.

Important Words

abolish (uh-BAHL-ish)—to put an end to something officially

compromise (KAHM-pruh-mize)—an agreement that is reached after people with opposing views each give up some of their demands

confederate (kuhn-FED-ur-it)—belonging to a union of people or nations

contrabands (KAHN-truh-bandz)—slaves who escaped to Union army lines

emancipation (i-man-suh-PAY-shuhn)—the freeing of a person or group from slavery or control

fugitive (FYOO-ji-tiv)—someone who is running away

homestead (HOME-sted)—to work land in exchange for being given the land

indentured (in-DENT-churd)—bound by an agreement to work for someone for a certain period of time

overseer (OH-vur-see-uhr)—a boss or supervisor

plantations (plan-TAY-shuhnz)—large farms found in warm climates, usually with a single main crop

seceded (suh-SEED-ed)—withdrew formally from a group or organization

slavers (SLAY-vuhrz)—people who sold and transported slaves

Index

Page numbers in **bold** indicate illustrations

About the Author

Jean F. Blashfield is the author of around 150 books, including several on the American Civil War. She has written about states, many different countries, historical events, chemistry, biology, and geology, and she created three encyclopedias for children. She was head of the book department at the company that produced Dungeons & Dragons® games and books. She has a degree from the University of Michigan and did graduate work at the University of Chicago. She lives in southern Wisconsin, though she has spent a great deal of her childhood in the South, where her ancestors grew cotton, pecans, sugarcane, and other crops grown by slaves.